USE BY PARENTS

As your child's first teacher, you are aware of the best way for your child to learn new information. Some children learn by performing large motor activities, such as hopping while saying a rhyme. Others enjoy quiet, manipulative work, such as putting a puzzle together.

Below is a variety of suggestions for ways the *Prekindergarten Holidays* pages can be used. The activities give you and your child quality time together, having fun and learning important skills. Generally, it is a good idea to make several copies of each page so that pictures can be cut apart and manipulated for continued use in games and activities. To keep the pieces together, store pictures and the Holiday Picture Flash Cards in envelopes. Mark envelopes holding the pictures from the same page with the holiday, and write the poem on the front for easy reference.

- Set up a specific place, such as a bulletin board, table, shelf, or area of the refrigerator, as the holiday center. Display pictures of items or the items themselves that represent the holiday. Review the items daily.

- Provide a large calendar. Have children glue or color holiday pictures in the appropriate square to show the date. Use the calendar to encourage math skills, such as counting down until the day, numeral recognition, and how to use the calendar.

- At appropriate times of the year, invite children to go on a holiday symbol hunt to find items associated with the celebration. A search can be done at home, while reading a book, or while riding in a car.

- Invite friends from other cultures to share their holiday traditions and food. Encourage them to display cultural dress and items indicative of their heritage. By celebrating cultural differences, children will appreciate the variety of people they see and meet.

- Find foods associated with the holidays for children to sample. The Internet is an excellent source of simple children's recipes that you and your child will enjoy cooking together.

- Find ways to incorporate the poem into the daily schedule. Make up motions for the poem for children to include as they say the rhyme. Poems can also be used for ideas to create art projects.

- To further enhance the key symbols from the poems and activity pages, read books that explore each holiday. Again, the Internet offers a large variety of child-friendly sites that have games and activities with which young children can safely interact.

- Have children color the pictures, then cut them out. Use the pictures to make flannel board pieces by sticking two-sided tape to the backs. A piece of felt can be laid on a table as the flannel board. As children say the rhymes, they can manipulate the pictures. Or, children can make up their own stories using the pictures. As children tell their stories, write them so that children can begin to see a connection between written and oral communication.

ACTIVITY CARD USES

The Holiday Picture Flash Cards and game board in the back of the book have multiple uses.

- Play Concentration. Children can match the picture sides of the Holiday Picture Flash Cards with a picture from the activity page.

- The Holiday Picture Flash Cards can also be used to play the game "A Year of Holidays" found on the fourth Activity Card. Children take turns rolling a number cube and moving a token, such as a penny, the spaces indicated. When children land on a picture, they should try to match a Holiday Picture Flash Card to the space they land on. Since some holidays have the same symbol, accept children's reasonable responses. Cards may end up uneven, but that is all right. All players must finish, but the player who has the most Holiday Picture Flash Cards wins.

- Discuss with your child important holidays and the meaningful traditions in which the family participates. Look through magazines to find pictures that could symbolize the celebration. Have your child use the pictures to tell a story on the Family Traditions Story Board.

USE BY TEACHERS

The pages in this book are designed as a fun way for children to experience different holidays and cultures. Since preschool children arrive in the classroom from a variety of cultures and with different experiences, it important that a teacher celebrate these many differences and explore them with sensitivity. It is important to remember that all children learn at different rates. Though some children seem totally oblivious to cultural differences, you never know when the interest may develop! Furthermore, children learn in different ways. For example, some learn by doing, whereas others learn by listening. Simply providing the information in a concrete, fun way and letting the children do what they will with the information is developmentally appropriate for this age.

It is a good idea to introduce a holiday one or two weeks before the actual celebration. Suggestions for activities, such as folder games and flannel board manipulatives, can be found in the Use by Parents section on page 1. Many of the ideas can be used for centers, small group work, or circle time. Ideas also offer a range of learning styles to ensure that children learn in a way that is comfortable and natural to them. Since children are exploring different cultures, food is always a fun and informative way to learn new information.

The following plan is a suggested format to introduce a holiday.

- Set up a holiday center. Include clothing, toys, symbols, and pictures to attract children's interest. Display a large calendar in the area.

- Gather the children in a circle and share two or three important items, preferably one that matches the picture on the Holiday Picture Flash Card. Relate small bits of background information. Some of the information in the Holiday Background Information is not important to the children. Choose only the information you think the children will enjoy. Be sure to allow time for children to share stories about the holiday or the item being shown.

- Explore the calendar daily to encourage math skill development. Glue a copy of or color the key picture symbol on the appropriate date. Count down the days until the festivities.

- Read aloud the poem identified at the end of the each holiday in the Holiday Background Information. Make up movements to accompany the poem. Encourage children to join in on repeated readings. Display the Holiday Picture Flash Card from the back of the book. Repeat the rhyme and identify the words or images in the poem associated with the holiday.

- Continue to read the poem, inviting children to join in. While transitioning to other activities or walking in the hall, say the poem.

- When studying a specific holiday, invite parents and guests to the classroom to share aspects of the holiday, such as food, clothing, games, and small symbols.

- Read the poem. After three or four days, pass out copies of the activity sheet. (You may want to write each child's name on the page beforehand.) Identify the pictures. Recite the poem aloud, and have children identify how the pictures relate to the poem and the holiday. Hold up the picture side of the Holiday Picture Flash Card so children can identify the last picture on the page. Invite children to color the pictures. Then, collect the pages.

- Review the poem and picture symbols. Read a holiday book. At the end of the week, send the activity page and a copy of the poem home with children.

BOOK SUGGESTIONS

- Drucker, Malka. *A Jewish Holiday ABC*. Gulliver Books, 1992.

- Most, Bernard. *Happy Holidaysaurus*. Harcourt Brace Children's Books, 1992.

- Price, Moe. *The Reindeer Christmas*. Harcourt Brace Children's Books, 1993.

- Yolen, Jane. *The Three Bears Holiday Rhyme Book*. Harcourt Brace Children's Books, 1995.

HOLIDAY BACKGROUND INFORMATION

Use these background descriptions and poems to encourage recognition of holidays. The page number following the holiday's name identifies the corresponding activity page.

New Year's Day, p. 9

New Year's Day is one of the oldest holidays. It was celebrated over 4,000 years ago in Babylon on March 23. The people chose that time because winter was over, and everything was beginning to grow. The Babylonians also started the tradition of making a New Year's resolution, but they resolved to return borrowed items. The Romans changed the date of the new year to January 1 after they adopted the Roman calendar. Some countries continue to follow the original date for celebrating New Year's Day. The symbol of the baby first appeared in Greece around 600 B.C. and represented rebirth. The Germans brought the symbol of the baby wearing a banner when they first came to America. It has long been the tradition to stay up until midnight to welcome the new year. The song, "Auld Lang Syne," originated in Scotland. The current lyrics were adopted in the 1700s, and then spread to many English-speaking countries. Food also has important significance in many cultures. Many people in America eat black-eyed peas and ham or hog jowls to bring them luck and prosperity for the coming year.

It's twelve o'clock; the New Year's here.
Blow your horn and give a cheer.

Martin Luther King, Jr., Day, p. 10

Martin Luther King, Jr., was born on January 15, 1929. He worked throughout his life to end segregation, the practice in which African-American people were forced to sit, work, eat, and play in separate areas. He led peaceful demonstrations and marches, often ending them with powerful speeches. He is most noted for his words, "I have a dream," in which he told a crowd about a vision he had for all people to be equal. He is credited for helping African Americans gain the right to vote and the right of children of all races to go to school together. He was given the Nobel Peace Prize in 1964 for his contributions to mankind. Dr. King was assassinated on April 4, 1968. In 1986, Congress passed a law to honor the work of Martin Luther King, Jr., on his birthday. It became a legal holiday in 1986 and has since been observed on the third Monday in January.

Martin Luther King, Jr., was a famous man,
Who had a special dream—
That people of all colors and beliefs
Would work as one big team.

Chinese New Year, p. 11

The Chinese New Year, also known as the Spring Festival, is the biggest holiday in China, Taiwan, and Hong Kong. It is celebrated anywhere from January 21 to February 19, depending on the lunar calendar, and lasts for fifteen days. It is a time of renewal. People get rid of old debts, clean their house, and buy new clothes. It is a big tradition that children receive red envelopes, which hold money. Fireworks are important in the celebration. Fireworks originated as a way to keep evil spirits away. Toward the end of the festival, dancers dress in animal costumes and tour the countryside. Bands with drums, cymbals, and gongs perform very loudly. Sticky cakes and sweet dumplings are favorite foods. Other snacks include dates, nuts, and oranges. The custom of the long dragon is an American variation that appears to have developed in San Francisco when waves of immigrants came to the new world. Kites are a popular children's toy that are also associated with the Chinese New Year. Many kites look like fish or lanterns, symbols of good luck, as they fly overhead.

A big, long dragon comes jumping down the street,
And the feet underneath step to the drum beat.
I get a red envelope—there's money inside.
What's best about Chinese New Year? I can't decide.

Groundhog Day, p. 12

Groundhog Day was first associated with the religious festival, Candlemas. It later became a secular ceremony celebrated before planting. The custom was first brought to America by German settlers. They believed that animals that hibernated came out periodically to check the weather. If the animal saw its shadow, six more weeks of bad weather would follow. If the animal did not see its shadow, spring was on its way. In Gobbler's Knob, Pennsylvania, each year on February 2, the townspeople celebrate Groundhog Day with a groundhog named Punxsutawney Phil. Since 1887, over 100 years, this groundhog has been forecasting the arrival of spring.

Groundhog sleeps all winter long,
But on February second he peeks
To tell if spring is coming soon
Or if winter lasts six more weeks.

www.svschoolsupply.com
© Steck-Vaughn Company

Prekindergarten Holidays, SV 2917-3

Valentine's Day, p. 13

Several stories, dating back to Roman civilization, tell the origins of Valentine's Day. The most popular is the story of the priest, Valentine, who performed secret marriages, even though the Roman law forbade single men to marry. Valentine was imprisoned and died in prison on February 14. The sending of cards became popular in Great Britain in the 1800s. Artists made elaborate cards showing children and flowers. Esther Howland first manufactured the cards in America. She decorated the cards with lace and paper flowers. In later years, Cupid, the winged son of Venus, became a popular symbol. Eventually the custom developed whereby flowers, candy, and cards were given as tokens of love on February 14.

Here's the paper, and here's the glue.
Here's the crayon to write "I Love You."
Make a card that you can send
On Valentine's Day to your best friend.

Hina Matsuri (Doll Festival), p. 14

Hina Matsuri is celebrated in Japan on March 3. The holiday honors young girls, and people pray for the health and happiness of girls they know. Dolls, often passed down through the mother, are set on a tiered display shelf covered with red felt. The dolls wear costumes associated with traditional Japanese noble dress. Peach blossoms, a symbol of Japan, are also included on the shelf with the dolls. The custom of using dolls originated because people believed that the dolls would protect the owner from bad luck and illness. Moreover, if someone touched a doll, the doll would take away everything that was bad. On Hina Matsuri, girls dress up in kimonos and visit each other. The dolls are offered diamond-shaped rice cakes. The cakes are then shared among family and friends.

In Japan there is a day that's just for little girls.
They put on a kimono—a kind of robe girls wear.
They ask their friends to visit to see their pretty dolls.
Then they pass the rice-cake treats that everyone will share.

Saint Patrick's Day, p. 15

Saint Patrick is the patron saint of Ireland. Tradition says that Patrick worked to convert the Irish to Christianity using a three-leaf shamrock to explain the Holy Trinity—the Father, Son, and Holy Ghost. Thus, Saint Patrick's Day is a religious holiday in Ireland and has long been celebrated on March 17. The Irish also have a long tradition of leprechauns who like to play pranks on mortals. Each leprechaun owns a pot of gold that is buried at the end of a rainbow. Irish immigrants brought the stories and holiday with them. The first Saint Patrick's Day was celebrated in America in 1737. The city of Boston organized a parade, and people wore green. The holiday quickly became a secular celebration.

Leprechauns and clover are signs of
Saint Patrick's most have seen,
But unless you want to get a pinch,
You should wear something green.

Pesach (Passover), p. 16

Pesach is a Jewish festival that celebrates the time over 3,000 years ago when the Israelites fled from slavery in Egypt. Passover refers to the night in which the Israelites marked their homes so that God would "pass over" their family and not kill the firstborn son. Passover is a time of sorrow in which Jews remember their slavery, but it is also a time of hope as they thank God for his power in releasing them from bondage, as well as his continued blessings in their lives. The holiday takes place in the spring during March or April, depending on the Jewish calendar, and lasts for eight days. Food is an important part of the holiday. Jews do not eat foods with leaven during this time. Leaven is the material in bread that makes it rise. The main source of bread is matzoh, a kind of flat cracker. On the night before the holiday, children are given a candle and a feather. They search each room to find leavened food. The feather helps them clean up what they find. The Passover celebration begins at sundown. During the first two nights, family and friends sit down to Seder, a meal served with special foods on special plates. A Seder plate is the center of the table and is divided into six parts. Each part holds a special kind of food that symbolizes the story of leaving Egypt. For example, a roasted, hardboiled egg is the symbol of new life. Bitter herbs or horseradish are a symbol of the hard times as slaves. Songs, prayers, and stories are also an important part of the festivities.

Here is a feather,
To sweep away bread crumbs.
Now get the Seder plate
Before Passover comes.

Divali (Diwali), p. 26

Divali is a Hindu New Year festival that lasts for five days in October or November and is one of the biggest celebrations in India. It is also known as the Festival of Lights, because people light small candles called divas, a bowl-like lamp filled with special oil. It is a symbol of welcome to the goddess Lakshmi, who brings blessings of wealth, health, and success in life. During this time, houses are thoroughly cleaned and intricate geometric patterns drawn on entryway floors. Business accounts, symbolized by a book, must be balanced and all debts repaid. Family and friends come together to feast on rice, curry, puri, a form of Indian bread, and ankoot, a sweet treat made from thickened milk.

Light the diva, clean the house,
Draw a pattern on the floor.
At Divali time we ask
For health and wealth once more.

Id-ul-Fitr, p. 27

Id-ul-Fitr is a Muslim holiday that takes place after Ramadan, a monthlong time when Muslims fast. During this time, they learn self-control, as well as practice performing good deeds. The dates for Ramadan and Id-ul-Fitr vary based on a Muslim lunar calendar. These holidays have started in January as well as in June. Id-ul-Fitr is a celebration to thank Allah for wealth and success in life. It cannot begin until the new moon is seen. Before Id begins, each person makes a payment, called zakat, to charity. The money goes to people who may not have enough money to pay for a big Id feast. On the morning of Id, people get up early and dress in new clothes. They go to the mosque, their place of worship. They give special Id cards, decorated with geometric patterns, flowers, or stars. No pictures of animals or people appear on the cards as Muslims never draw these images since they believe no one can copy Allah's creation. Muslims also exchange small presents, such as dried fruit. Everyone eats a big celebration dinner. Most people prepare a special sweet pudding made from rice.

The new moon is up; it's time for Id.
First, we'll go to the mosque to pray.
Then I'll give you a card filled with best wishes,
And we'll eat a big feast today.

Thanksgiving Day, p. 28

Thanksgiving Day is the American holiday that remembers the Pilgrim feast of 1621. It had been a good harvest for the Pilgrims. Governor William Bradford proclaimed a feast that would last for three days. American Indians were invited since they were the people who showed the Pilgrims which seeds to plant and how to grow the vegetables. The pilgrims and 90 American Indians came together to play games and eat. They served such foods as duck, turkey, cornbread, vegetables, and corn pudding. The feast was not repeated by the colonists. In 1789, George Washington proclaimed November 26 as a public day of thanksgiving and prayer. Many states celebrated it annually after that point. President Abraham Lincoln later proclaimed the last Thursday in November as Thanksgiving Day. Finally, in 1939, President Franklin Roosevelt changed the date to the fourth Thursday in November in an effort to give store merchants more time to sell for the Christmas season. Congress made the date permanent soon after.

People think of Pilgrims when
Thanksgiving Day is near.
But I only think of pumpkin pie—
Please pass a slice right here.

Hanukkah, p. 29

Hanukkah, also known as the Festival of Lights, dates to over 2,000 years ago when the Syrians ruled Israel. The Jews were forced to worship Greek gods. A small group of Jews rebelled and fought the huge Syrian army. After winning, the Jews began to cleanse their temple. To make it holy once more, the Jews needed to rededicate the temple to God. They found the menorah, a nine-branch candleholder, and enough oil to burn for one day. By a miracle of God, the oil lasted eight days and nights. From that time, Hanukkah has been observed on the 25th day of Kislev, a Jewish calendar month. The holiday falls in November or December. The celebration begins at sunset. Each night, the family lights one candle on the menorah until all eight candles are lit. The ninth candle is the helper candle and lights the eight candles. The whole family gathers around and says a prayer. Afterwards, they eat the meal together. Potato latkes and doughnuts are favored foods, since they are made with oil. Children also play the dreidel game. The dreidel is a four-sided spinning top with a Jewish letter on each side.

Here's a dreidel just for you,
And potato latkes, too.
Light eight candles—one each night
To keep Hanukkah burning bright.

Christmas, p. 30

Christmas began as a Christian holiday celebrating the birth of Jesus Christ. It has long been observed on December 25, although the actual date of Jesus' birth is unknown. Many countries around the world celebrate it as a secular day, but the implications of goodwill and peace are still the same. In all countries, presents are exchanged. Different countries have different individuals who deliver the gifts. In the United States, Santa Claus rides in a sleigh to deliver toys. The actual figure of Santa Claus came from Saint Nicholas, a bishop who performed kind deeds for the poor. The idea of Santa Claus came to the United States from Holland and evolved into the character who wears red clothing. The Christmas tree is a custom that came from Germany. Germans decorated evergreens with candles, to stand for stars. The bell symbol comes from Europe. Bells were rung to ward off bad spirits. Over the years, a bell symbolized ringing out the happy news of Christ's birth. The candy cane was the product of a candy maker. He made white candy sticks into the shape of a shepherd's crook to symbolize Christ as the good shepherd.

Christmas lights are everywhere.
The star is on the tree.
When will Santa ride his sleigh
And come to visit me?

Kwanzaa, p. 31

Kwanzaa, which means "first fruits of the harvest" in Kiswahili, is an African-American celebration that begins December 26 and lasts for seven days. Begun by Dr. Maulana Ron Karenga in 1966, it is a holiday in which African Americans think about their African heritage and celebrate the values of family, community, responsibility, commerce, and self-improvement. The colors are very symbolic: red stands for blood that the people shed, black for the face of the people, and green for hope. The kinara is a candleholder that holds seven candles; three green, three red, and one black. The table setting is very important. A woven mat is used to symbolize the heritage of the culture. Fruits and vegetables symbolize harvest. Corn is also set out, one ear for each child in the family. Other traditions include the exchange of homemade gifts. Family and friends sit down to a huge feast on December 31 and share their feelings about the holiday and family.

Set out the mat and kinara.
Add an ear of corn,
For at Kwanzaa there should be
One for each child born.

Birthdays, p. 32

Though not a true holiday, birthdays are the biggest event in a child's life. Some of the customs for a birthday date back thousands of years. The birthday crown may have originated because kings were the only ones able to celebrate birthdays at one time. Parties started in Europe because people believed that evil spirits were attracted to those having a birthday. Friends and family would gather to bring good thoughts and wishes to scare away the spirits. They often brought presents to further express good cheer. The tradition of the birthday cake started in Germany. People would bake small tokens, such as coins and thimbles, in cakes. As people got the cake slices, the token would predict the future. For example, a person finding a coin in the cake would be prosperous. Candles also are part of German tradition. They would put a candle on a cake for each year the person lived. One more was put on to provide hope that the person would live another year. The "Happy Birthday" song is the most popular song in the world. It is sung in almost every language in the world. It is over 100 years old.

All my friends have come today.
"Happy Birthday," they scream.
Soon they'll sing the birthday song,
Then eat some cake and ice cream.

Name _____

NEW YEAR'S DAY

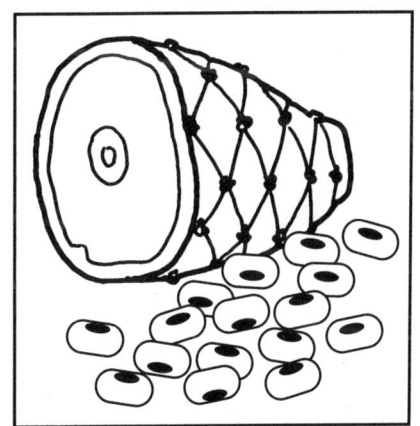

Use the information on page 3 to tell children about New Year's Day. Read aloud the poem, inviting children to join in on repeated readings. Then, have children identify and color the pictures.

New Year's Day, p. 3

www.svschoolsupply.com
© Steck-Vaughn Company

Prekindergarten Holidays, SV 2917-3

Name _____

MARTIN LUTHER KING, JR., DAY

MLK, Jr., Day, p. 3

Use the information on page 3 to tell children about Martin Luther King, Jr., Day. Read aloud the poem, inviting children to join in on repeated readings. Then, have children identify and color the pictures.

www.svschoolsupply.com
© Steck-Vaughn Company

Prekindergarten Holidays, SV 2917-3

Name _____

CHINESE NEW YEAR

Chinese New Year, p. 3

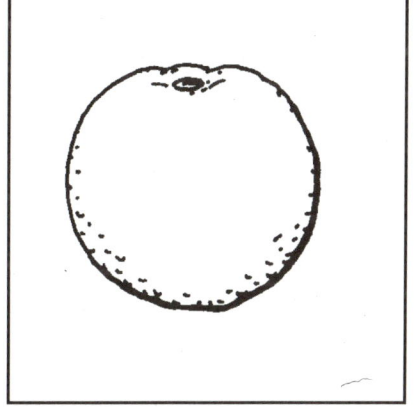

Use the information on page 3 to tell children about Chinese New Year. Read aloud the poem, inviting children to join in on repeated readings. Then, have children identify and color the pictures.

www.svschoolsupply.com
© Steck-Vaughn Company

Prekindergarten Holidays, SV 2917-3

Name _____

GROUNDHOG DAY

Groundhog Day, p. 3

Use the information on page 3 to tell children about Groundhog Day. Read aloud the poem, inviting children to join in on repeated readings. Then, have children identify and color the pictures.

www.svschoolsupply.com
© Steck-Vaughn Company

Prekindergarten Holidays, SV 2917-3

Name _____

VALENTINE'S DAY

Valentine's Day, p. 4

Use the information on page 4 to tell children about Valentine's Day. Read aloud the poem, inviting children to join in on repeated readings. Then, have children identify and color the pictures.

www.svschoolsupply.com

© Steck-Vaughn Company

Prekindergarten Holidays, SV 2917-3

Name _____

HINA MATSURI (Doll Festival)

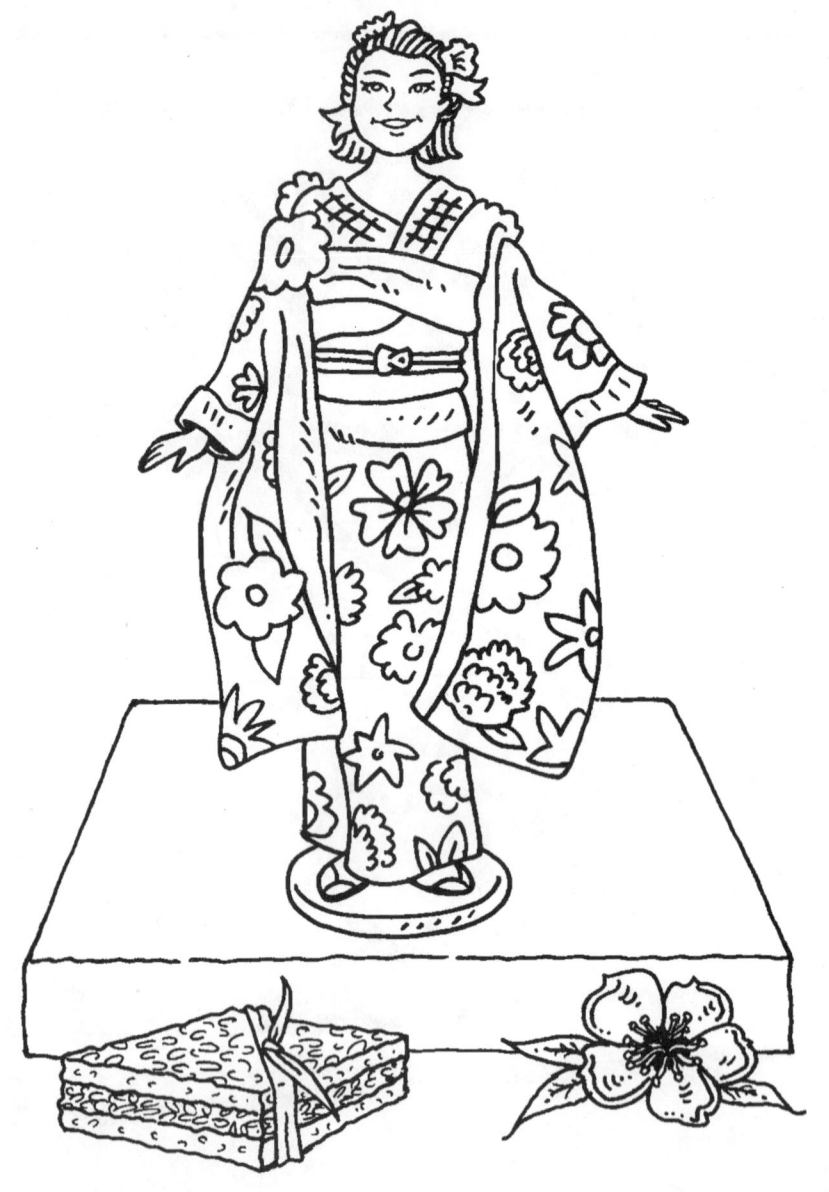

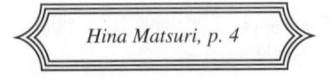

Hina Matsuri, p. 4

Use the information on page 4 to tell children about Hina Matsuri. Read aloud the poem, inviting children to join in on repeated readings. Then, have children identify and color the pictures.

www.svschoolsupply.com
© Steck-Vaughn Company

14

Prekindergarten Holidays, SV 2917-3

Name _____

SAINT PATRICK'S DAY

Saint Patrick's Day, p. 4

Use the information on page 4 to tell children about Saint Patrick's Day. Read aloud the poem, inviting children to join in on repeated readings. Then, have children identify and color the pictures.

www.svschoolsupply.com
© Steck-Vaughn Company

Prekindergarten Holidays, SV 2917-3

Name _____

PESACH (Passover)

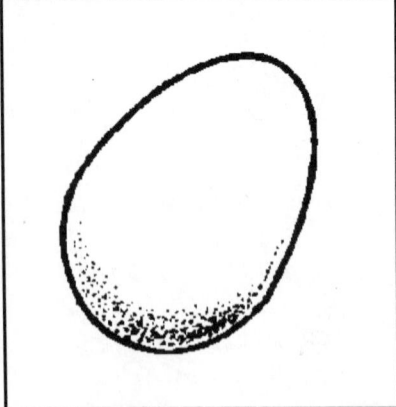

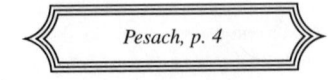

Pesach, p. 4

Use the information on page 4 to tell children about Pesach. Read aloud the poem, inviting children to join in on repeated readings. Then, have children identify and color the pictures.

www.svschoolsupply.com
© Steck-Vaughn Company

16

Prekindergarten Holidays, SV 2917-3

Name _____

EASTER

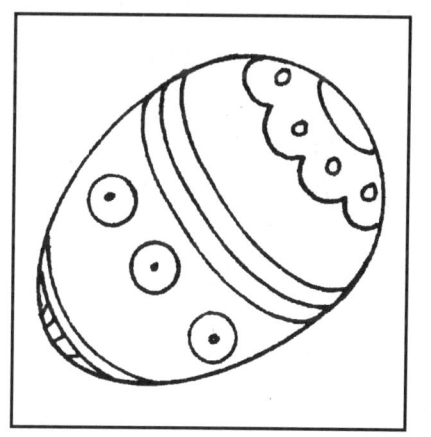

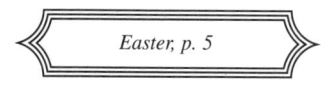

Easter, p. 5

Use the information on page 5 to tell children about Easter. Read aloud the poem, inviting children to join in on repeated readings. Then, have children identify and color the pictures.

www.svschoolsupply.com
© Steck-Vaughn Company

17

Prekindergarten Holidays, SV 2917-3

Name _____

EARTH DAY

Earth Day, p. 5

Use the information on page 5 to tell children about Earth Day. Read aloud the poem, inviting children to join in on repeated readings. Then, have children identify and color the pictures.

www.svschoolsupply.com
© Steck-Vaughn Company

Prekindergarten Holidays, SV 2917-3

Name _____

KODOMO NO HI (Children's Day)

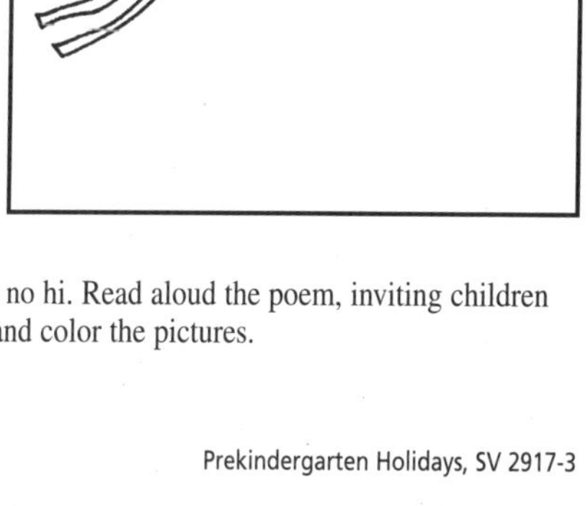

Kodomo no hi, p. 5

Use the information on page 5 to tell children about Kodomo no hi. Read aloud the poem, inviting children to join in on repeated readings. Then, have children identify and color the pictures.

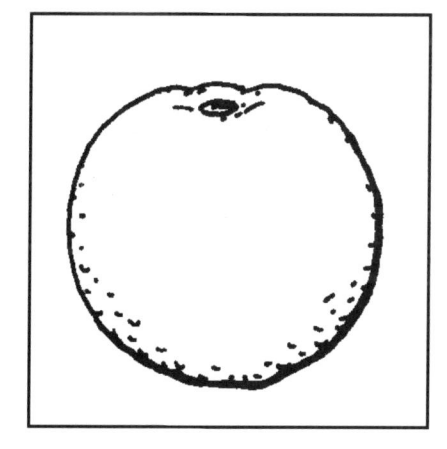

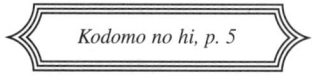

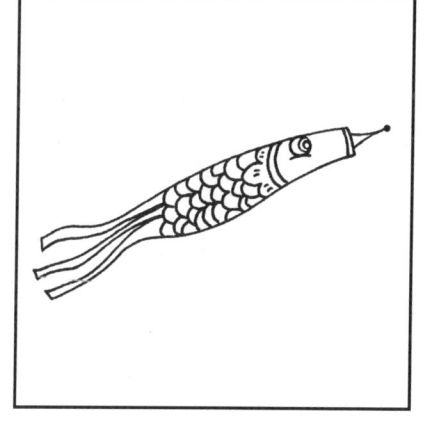

www.svschoolsupply.com
© Steck-Vaughn Company

Prekindergarten Holidays, SV 2917-3

Name _____

CINCO DE MAYO

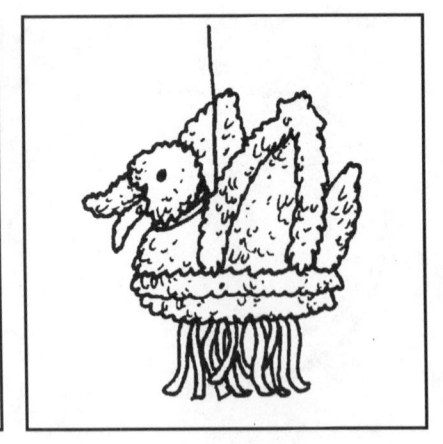

Cinco de Mayo, p. 5

Use the information on page 5 to tell children about Cinco de Mayo. Read aloud the poem, inviting children to join in on repeated readings. Then, have children identify and color the pictures.

www.svschoolsupply.com
© Steck-Vaughn Company

Prekindergarten Holidays, SV 2917-3

Name _____

MOTHER'S DAY

Mother's Day, p. 6

Use the information on page 6 to tell children about Mother's Day. Read aloud the poem, inviting children to join in on repeated readings. Then, have children identify and color the pictures.

Name _____

MEMORIAL DAY

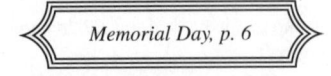

Memorial Day, p. 6

Use the information on page 6 to tell children about Memorial Day. Read aloud the poem, inviting children to join in on repeated readings. Then, have children identify and color the pictures.

Name _____

FATHER'S DAY

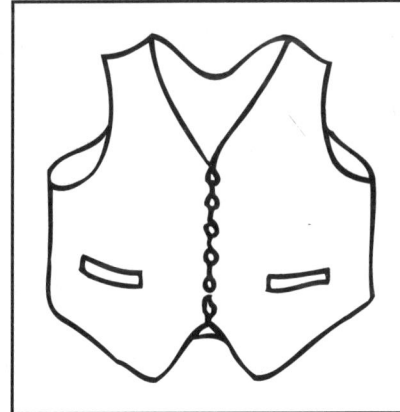

Father's Day, p. 6

Use the information on page 6 to tell children about Father's Day. Read aloud the poem, inviting children to join in on repeated readings. Then, have children identify and color the pictures.

www.svschoolsupply.com
© Steck-Vaughn Company

Prekindergarten Holidays, SV 2917-3

Name _____

INDEPENDENCE DAY (July 4th)

Independence Day, p. 6

Use the information on page 6 to tell children about July Fourth. Read aloud the poem, inviting children to join in on repeated readings. Then, have children identify and color the pictures.

Name _____

CHEROKEE NATIONAL HOLIDAY

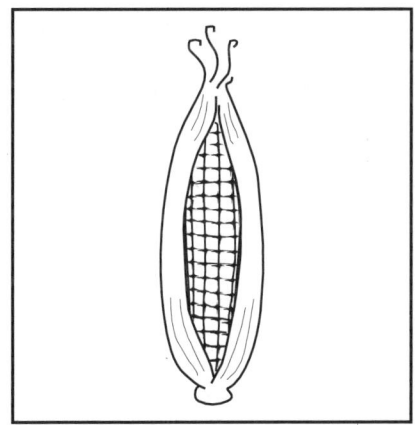

Cherokee Holiday, p. 6

Use the information on page 6 to tell children about Cherokee National Holiday. Read aloud the poem, inviting children to join in on repeated readings. Then, have children identify and color the pictures.

www.svschoolsupply.com

© Steck-Vaughn Company

Prekindergarten Holidays, SV 2917-3

Name _____

DIVALI

Divali, p. 7 — Use the information on page 7 to tell children about Divali. Read aloud the poem, inviting children to join in on repeated readings. Then, have children identify and color the pictures.

www.svschoolsupply.com
© Steck-Vaughn Company

Prekindergarten Holidays, SV 2917-3

Name _____

ID-UL-FITR

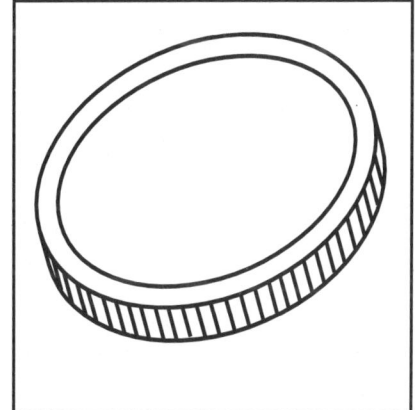

Id-ul-Fitr, p. 7

Use the information on page 7 to tell children about Id-ul-Fitr. Read aloud the poem, inviting children to join in on repeated readings. Then, have children identify and color the pictures.

Name _____

THANKSGIVING DAY

Thanksgiving Day, p. 7

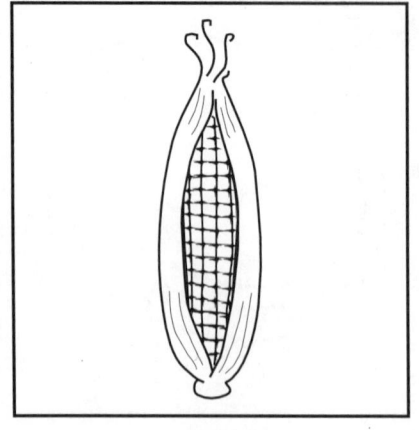

Use the information on page 7 to tell children about Thanksgiving Day. Read aloud the poem, inviting children to join in on repeated readings. Then, have children identify and color the pictures.

Name _____

HANUKKAH

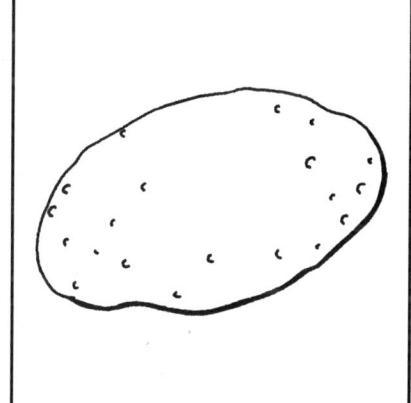

Hanukkah, p. 7

Use the information on page 7 to tell children about Hanukkah. Read aloud the poem, inviting children to join in on repeated readings. Then, have children identify and color the pictures.

Name _____

CHRISTMAS

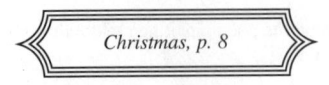

Christmas, p. 8

Use the information on page 8 to tell children about Christmas. Read aloud the poem, inviting children to join in on repeated readings. Then, have children identify and color the pictures.

www.svschoolsupply.com
© Steck-Vaughn Company

Prekindergarten Holidays, SV 2917-3

Name _____

KWANZAA

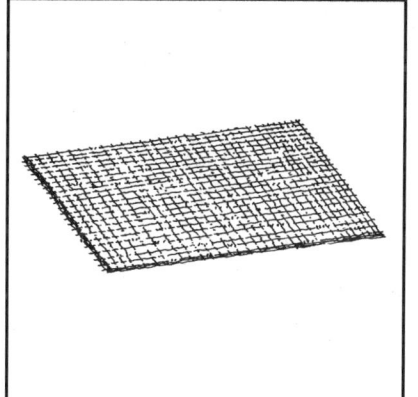

Kwanzaa, p. 8

Use the information on page 8 to tell children about Kwanzaa. Read aloud the poem, inviting children to join in on repeated readings. Then, have children identify and color the pictures.

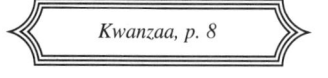

Name _____

BIRTHDAYS

Birthdays, p. 8

Use the information on page 8 to tell children about birthdays. Read aloud the poem, inviting children to join in on repeated readings. Then, have children identify and color the pictures.

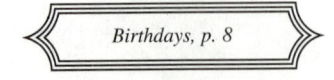

www.svschoolsupply.com
© Steck-Vaughn Company

Prekindergarten Holidays, SV 2917-3